MY FIRST COOKBOOK EASY RECIPES FOR KIDS AGES 4-6

Growing Chefs Building Healthy Habits through Cooking

By

Amelia Richardson

ABOUT THE AUTHOR

Amelia Richardson is a professional chef who is committed to cooking and serving delicious food while supporting a healthy approach to eating. With years of expertise in the food industry, Amelia knows how to bring a fun and knowledgeable approach to the kitchen. As a parent herself, Amelia comprehends the significance of familiarizing kids with the art of cooking early on. "My First Cookbook Easy Recipes for Kids Ages 4-6" is a wonderful creation developed out of Amelia's dedication to empowering little chefs and building an eternal passion for healthy and tasty eating.

CONTENTS

INTRODUCTION

There is something truly beautiful about cooking with kids! It takes me back to my childhood days, standing on a flimsy chair at the kitchen counter, wearing my mother's oversized apron, passionately mixing and measuring ingredients. And, of course, the greatest reward was always getting to lick the spoon!

Now, as a parent to two little angels, I have carried on the custom of cooking with my toddlers. Undoubtedly, there were times when I required more than just a sprinkle of patience with my little helpers.

Yet, amidst the occasional chaos and mess, the kitchen has remained a place of laughter, learning, joy, and cherished memories for me and my kids.

Teaching kids how to cook is a priceless gift we can offer them, and believe me, it is never too late to start. Their enthusiastic determination to "I want to make it myself" is not only cute but also highly empowering because, with little patience, they truly can master how to cook independently! I felt a sense of achievement when my kids, all under the age of six, took charge of our easy breakfast dishes. Sure, it did not always go as planned, but the sense of confidence and pride shining in their eyes when they showed their food creations was extremely priceless to me as a mother.

Now, with my latest cookbook, "My First Cookbook Easy Recipes for Kids Ages 4-6," I am delighted to provide a pathway to spark a lifelong love for food and cooking for kids. Every recipe is delightfully simple, with step-by-step directions.

From rolling and whisking to stirring and squeezing, little chefs will have fun perfecting basic kitchen skills in a whole new way. They will discover the happiness of kneading dough, mixing batter, cracking eggs, and exploring a rainbow of ingredients - all of these items you probably have at home already! Whether it's hearty breakfasts, lunches, dinners, whole snacks, or lovely desserts, I have crafted the recipes with the intention of uniting the whole family in the pleasure of cooking and eating together. So, get yourself ready for a cooking adventure filled with flavor, fun, and lots of laughter!

CHAPTER 1: GETTING STARTED IN THE KITCHEN

Welcome to the thrilling world of cooking adventures, where little chefs will set off on a delectable adventure full of fun, happiness, and tasty dishes! Let's go right into the core of the kitchen in this chapter and examine every little detail to guarantee our cooking adventures are as smooth as frosting on the cake.

1.1 NOTE TO PARENTS

Greetings! I am Amelia - a professional chef, mom, and the creator of the book "My First Cookbook Easy Recipes for Kids Ages 4-6." It is astonishing how life throws surprises our way. I never guessed I'd be teaching kids how to cook. Back in the past, cooking with kids was full of stress for me. I spent three hours on dinner only to end up with something uninspiring. But this has changed with time, and cooking with kids has become my happy and fun time.

In the kitchen, surrounded by pleasant aromas, lies an amazing chance to connect with your kids and your heritage. The kitchen is the place where you can share your household recipes, narrate tales from past generations, and make new memories while honoring age-old traditions. Trying recipes related to your cultural background can also be an amusing way to familiarize your kids with their roots.

By letting them hold the whisk, you are not only teaching your kids how to cook, but you are also building confidence in them. And there is no better place to begin than with this cookbook! The recipes within are not only easy and tasty but also contain all five flavors sensed by the human tongue:

- Sour

- Sweet

- Bitter

- Salty

- Savory

When gathered around the dinner table, the act of eating food together not only nourishes our bodies but also strengthens family bonds, sharing the happiness and comfort of food, spending time with family, and feeling a sense of security and encouragement. Who could resist indulging in such a delicious offering?

Cooking for kids can be educational and fun at the same time. It can assist in building self-esteem and boost the likelihood of a kid experiencing something new. Cooking is a healthy activity for kids, and it requires some preparations before getting started. For maximum fun and minimal worry, keep the following things in mind:

- Keep the Schedule in Mind: Remember that the kitchen activity takes time and attention. If you are in a hurry, there will be no fun. Preparation and cooking times are estimated for an adult cooking the dish. Kids often require more time, so it is crucial to consider that.

- Cooking is a Truly Sensory Experience: You should encourage the kids to taste ingredients as they cook. A kid who may be hesitant to try new food at the dining table might find it much easier to taste the same ingredient while making the food themselves. This lack of pressure to eat can make a picky eater feel more inclined to discover new flavors. Additionally, it is great to have additional ingredients available for this purpose.

- Step Backward When Needed: Just like learning to walk and read is a process for kids, learning how to cook is the same. Kids will make mistakes in the kitchen, as well as in life, and it is important for their growth. If there isn›t an urgent safety issue, allow kids to make these mistakes. It is a way for them to learn. So, do not try to be a backseat critic!

- Cleanup as You Proceed: While you are busy in the kitchen, why not enjoy a tune and clean up the dishes as you proceed? Engage the kids in the process of cleaning to avoid having a chaotic kitchen later. Plus, cleaning up together after cooking provides kids with more exposure to new ingredients, potentially making them more open to trying that food when it is served.

- Don't Be So High on Expectations: Parenting usually revolves around having higher expectations, and cooking is no exception. Keep your kid›s attention span in mind. It is crucial to discuss the recipe before getting started. How much time will the cooking require? How much time does it require to bake and cool before we can have it? It is completely okay if a recipe isn›t going as well as planned. Allow your child to play around in the backyard while you complete it. Let›s try it another day. Similar to any other activity, there are times when you have to make a change.

- Embrace the Beauty of imperfection: It may not come out perfect, but it is perfect for your little one. The sense of achievement and pride that comes with «I cooked it myself,» is completely priceless. Besides, a delicious mess is still delightful.

- Begin Slowly: If your kid is stepping into the kitchen for the first time, begin with easier recipes and let them polish their skills as you try recipes through this book. Remember, the ultimate goal is a delicious meal and a wonderful smile.

- Turn Your Little One into a Chef: Nothing is built overnight, correct? The more you cook with your kid, the better you will be at taking a step back, and your kid's cooking skills will improve. **Nothing will give you more happiness than a meal cooked by your happy little chef.**

"My First Cookbook Easy Recipes for Kids Ages 4-6" aims to provide your kid with the confidence and self-esteem to take over the kitchen and cook by themselves. Begin by following the easy recipes and make your way towards the medium or hard as your kid's cooking skills grow. Begin by reading out "A Note to Little Chefs" for your kids, which is the next section of this chapter. Take a walk through your kitchen together, guiding your kid to where the necessary kitchen equipment is. Read through all the introductory chapters of this book and discuss together the rules for the kitchen, tips, measurements, kitchen terminologies, and tools. Whenever adult assistance is needed — since small kids cannot handle tasks such as stoves, cutting, or hot surfaces all by themselves — your help is essential to complete the process and ensure their safety. This includes tasks like taking out the hot pan from the oven or cutting with a sharp knife.

If your kid is able to read, you can give this book to them and go rest — within hearing distance. This book aims to promote independence, and the reading kid is prepared for that step.

Remember, kids can be impulsive. If you give them this book, it is likely to spark their interest, and they will want to do the cooking immediately. Make sure to pick your timing carefully.

And finally, enjoy yourself! Remember, cooking is all about fun, happiness, and laughter.

1.2 NOTE TO LITTLE CHEFS

Are you aware of your cooking abilities, little chefs? You truly have the skills, and you are about to demonstrate them. Whether you are just stepping into the kitchen for the first time or have an idea of how to cook, this book is designed especially for you.

Every recipe in this book is rated with a difficulty level of Easy, Medium or Hard. This is for your convenience, so you can see how much you can do on your own. However, please keep in mind that adult assistance will be necessary throughout the cooking process, which indicates that you should ask your parents to step in for help. This can be a bit hard, but I want you to be completely safe.

To be on the safer side next time, remember to write notes and don't completely rely on your memory because sometimes, it is hard to remember what we have done before. So do not make the same mistake again and again, and write notes about every recipe:

- **Who helped you in cooking?**

- **Did you like the recipe?**

- **Did you make any changes to the recipe while preparing it?**

Cooking is not just about being serious all the time — it is about adding a pinch of laughter to every recipe! So, are you ready to whip up something tasty? Let's get cooking!

DIFFICULTY LEVELS

Every recipe is categorized into 3 levels: Easy, Medium or Hard to give you a sense of understanding of how hard or easy it is and how much adult assistance is needed.

- **Easy: Recipes at this level are easy, quick, and delicious.**

- **Medium: Recipes at this level are a bit difficult and require some effort, but you will do it, so don't worry. Remember to ask your parents for help if needed.**

- **Hard: Recipes at this level have more ingredients and steps. Make these with your parents, but just make sure you are leading.**

1.3 HOW TO USE THE RECIPES IN THIS BOOK (FOR KIDS)

Hey, little chefs! Do you know that cooking from the recipes written in this book is a 3-way process? If you prepare your ingredients ahead of cooking time, and organize cooking tools before you begin making dishes, the possibility of mistakes will diminish. You won't be lost digging around your kitchen for tools and ingredients while food is being cooked on the stove or in the oven. Here are the 3 steps that you are required to follow:

1. PREPARE YOUR INGREDIENTS

First, go through the ingredient list and prepare them as per instructions. Measure the ingredients as directed in the recipe. Clean veggies and fruits and organize ingredients in the preparation bowls.

2. GATHER COOKING TOOLS

When you are done preparing your ingredients, the next step is to gather all the cooking tools required for the recipe on your kitchen counter.

3. BEGIN COOKING

Finally, start making your food. Keep your mobile or other toys out of the kitchen, and keep other chores for later. Keep all your emphasis on the cooking now!

1.4 RULES FOR THE KITCHEN (FOR KIDS)

The kitchen is the place where magic happens; delicious dishes are created, tempting aromas dominate the air, and a memorable time is shared through laughter and smiles. When it comes to preparing food, some general rules should be followed. Further, parents can also add a few rules to this list, so make sure to check them.

ASK FOR PARENTS' ASSISTANCE

Keep in mind that throughout the cooking process, adult assistance is necessary; it means your parents need to help or supervise you. A few steps may need a bit more assistance than others, like using the stove or handling the sharp food processor. You might also need a helping hand when taking something hot out of the oven. Keep in mind that a great chef always asks for help when necessary.

REMEMBER TO WASH YOUR HANDS

The initial step before preparing meals is to wash your hands. The next step is to ensure that you don't touch your nose. It's unhygienic, and anything that is on your hands will stick to it or vice versa, so begin with clean and tidy hands. Wash your hands under warm water twice and soap them between the fingers and nails, too, to clean them properly.

CLEAN VEGGIES AND FRUITS

Veggies and fruits come from the soil and different locations before coming to your kitchen counter. Even before cutting or peeling anything, it is best to wash it anyway. Water is commonly enough to wash them properly.

SAFELY HANDLE MEAT AND EGGS

Few raw foods are safer to handle than the others. For instance, if you are using raw meat and eggs, make sure to begin with clean hands and a neat workspace. Right after touching raw meat or eggs, wash your hands. Then, clean your workspace and chopping board well before putting anything else in the same spot. Remember to keep two cutting boards, one for meat and the other for everything else.

GET YOUR WORKSPACE READY

Before you begin cooking, wipe down your workspace using a damp, clean cloth. Also, ensure you have enough space available for working.

Set yourself up so that your belly aligns with your workspace. If you don't have a learning tower or another safe way to reach the height of the counter, consider arranging up a workspace on the floor. For that, lay out a clean towel or blanket and set up your ingredients and tools over it.

KEEP THINGS CLEAN AS YOU WORK

In order to keep your kitchen tidy and avoid having a stack of dirty dishes waiting for you in the sink, clean your equipment and tools as you work. If something is baking in the oven or your prepared meal is cooling down, wash untidy dishes to kill time.

As we are ending this crucial chapter of kitchen adventures, our cooking journey is far from over! Let's jump into our next interesting and important chapter, which is the most crucial one to understand and learn all the basics of the kitchen. From understanding kitchen ingredients, measurements, and kitchen terminologies to exploring kitchen tools and equipment, we will equip our little chefs with everything they require to win the battle of the kitchen confidently. So, let's jump straight into the next chapter and continue our cooking adventures together!

CHAPTER 2: KITCHEN ESSENTIALS FOR LITTLE CHEFS

Welcome, little chefs, to a chapter loaded with kitchen wonders! In this chapter, we will dive into the thrilling world of cooking essentials, where every spatula, whisk, and sprinkle of flour is a step toward culinary mastery. So, wear your chef hats and get ready to embark on an informative journey filled with kitchen terminology, ingredients, measurements, tools, and a drizzle of cooking magic!

2.1 UNDERSTANDING KITCHEN TERMINOLOGY

Hey, little chefs! Learning the kitchen language is like learning a foreign language. I know it can often be troubling to understand all the words used in the recipes. Here is your reference guide to navigate through this challenge. Let's look at some of the most common words used in cooking and their actual meanings.

Baking: It means to cook dishes inside the oven.

Batter: A mixture made using ingredients like sugar, flour, eggs, and water that is utilized in preparing pancakes, cookies, and cakes.

Beating: It means mixing thoroughly and hard with a fork, whisk, electric mixer, or spoon.

Blending: It means mixing ingredients together until creamy.

Boiling: Boiling means to cook liquid/fluid until the bubbles emerge on the surface and hit the boiling point, which is around 212°F/100°C.

Broiling: It means to keep your food under the broiler of the oven, where the dish heats up from the top.

Chopping: Chopping means to cut veggies, food, or other items into small-sized portions using a knife.

Dicing: It means to cut food into equal-sized, small, square pieces.

Drain: It means to remove the liquid from the stored or cooked food.

Drizzle: It means to sprinkle drops of items, like chocolate syrup or icing, lightly over the top of your food, like cookies and cake.

Fold: It means to gently mix together the ingredients from all sides until they are just mixed together.

Grate: Grating means to shred your ingredients into tiny bits using a food processor, blender, shredder, or grater.

Melt: It means to heat the solid food, such as, butter on the stovetop or in the microwave until it becomes liquid.

Peeling: It means to remove the outer skin, rind, or layer from your food, like fruit or veggies. This is often conducted using a vegetable peeler.

Scrape: It means pushing ingredients to the sides of a bowl, blender, pan, food processor, or jar, or back into the center. Always use a rubber spatula to perform this.

Simmering: Simmering means heating the liquids/fluids until small bubbles emerge, such as when cooking soup.

Slice: It means to cut food using a knife with 2 flat sides, with the thickness noted in the recipes.

Shredding: Shredding means cutting food like veggies or cheese into uniform, tiny pieces with the shredding disk or grater.

Stirring: It means to mix ingredients inside a cooking vessel or bowl, usually with the help of a rubber spatula or wooden spoon.

Toast: It means to heat up the slices of bread or nuts in a toaster, oven, or skillet until golden or light brown and fragrant.

Toss: Tossing means gently mixing the ingredients using two forks or tongs to distribute them evenly. Like you toss the salad, you do not mix it.

Whisking: It means to mix ingredients with a whisk, like whisking eggs prior to cooking them.

Whipping: It means to combine ingredients vigorously using a whisk to add air and double the volume of the ingredients, like whipping cream or egg whites.

Zest: It means to remove the outer colored peel from lemon or orange; the colored skin is called zest. This does not include the inner white layer known as pith.

2.2 KITCHEN UTENSILS AND TOOLS YOU WILL NEED

Having the correct sort of tools when preparing meals is like having a life-saving jacket. Visualize it as if you were trying to make a mountain of spaghetti in a small pan - disastrous, correct? So, let's learn about cooking lifesavers; I mean necessary cooking appliances and tools, divided into 5 outstanding categories, including small appliances, kitchen basics, cookware, cooking tools, and preparation tools.

And yes, you might need unique lifesavers for certain recipes, like a cupcake tray! Are you ready, little chefs? Let's jump into this:

1. PREPARATION TOOLS

- **Knives:** These are essential for slicing and dicing different ingredients for cooking.

- **Box Grater:** This multitasking tool converts solid ingredients into fine shreds and gratings.

- **Chopping Board:** This is the sturdy foundation for your food creations; it assists in protecting your countertops from cutting dents while you cut your ingredients on the chopping board.

- **Dry Measuring Cups:** These cups assist in ensuring the right balance of dry items.

- **Measuring Spoons:** These small kitchen spoons help you add the correct amount of ingredients to your meals.

- **Liquid Measuring Cups:** These cups assist in measuring accurate liquid concoctions for ideal recipes.

- **Vegetable Peeler:** This slick tool assists in shredding the outer covers of veggies to expose their amazing inside.

- **Ruler:** This is important for measuring dough and other kitchen tasks accurately.

- Can Opener: This aids in opening various store-bought canned things.

- Salad Spinner: This tool assists in crisping up your salad greens for a delicious salad encore.

- Citrus Juicer: This tool assists in pressing the lemons to bring a burst of flavor into your recipes.

- Garlic Press: This assists in extracting the garlic stuff in order to give a fantastic flavor to your dishes.

2. SMALL APPLIANCES

- Blender: This smooth operator is necessary for blending everything from creamy soups to silky smoothies.

- Microwave: This quick gadget is crucial for heating different ingredients used in many recipes or simply reheating your food.

- Toaster: This morning hero helps to turn the bread slices into crunchy, golden toast for your favorite spreads.

- Electric Mixer: This baking expert aids in whipping up creams and batters for delectable desserts with effortless relief.

- Food Processor: This gadget assists with chopping, dicing, and slicing different ingredients.

3. COOKWARE

- Large Saucepan: The most suitable pot to make gravy, sauces, and soups.

- Non-Stick Skillet: The main equipment of breakfasts, perfect for making eggs or making or flipping pancakes without facing the sticking scenario.

- Metal Skillet: The cooking pot for searing meats and stir-fries.

- Baking Pan: The best pan for making casseroles and gooey brownies.

- Muffin Tray: Your baking companion for creating cute and bite-sized treats, from savory cupcakes to muffins.

- Cooling Rack: The kitchen superhero that saves your treats from getting soggy, making sure they are cooled to crispy and crunchy perfection.

- Rimmed Baking Sheet: This is an excellent tool for roasting veggies and baking cookies.

4. KITCHEN BASICS

- Prep Bowls (large, small, and medium sizes): Your best partner for organizing and assembling ingredients before you begin cooking.

- Dish Towels: This cleanup friend helps to tackle spills, cushion hot pots, and clean hands.

- Plastic Wrap: This is excellent for wrapping up leftovers in order to preserve their freshness.

- Oven Mitts: They safeguard your hands when handling the heated stove or oven.

- Aluminum Foil: This helps protect your meals from heat and provides effortless cleanup.

- Paper Towels: This is the immediate solution for easy cleanup, wiping, and dabbing in the kitchen.

5. COOKING TOOLS

- Instant-Read Thermometer: This tool guarantees your dishes are cooked to perfection by checking their temperature.

- Rubber Spatula: This is used to scrape bowls clean and ensure no residue is left behind.

- Wooden Spoon: This is essential for mixing and tasting different recipes during cooking.

- Whisk: This maestro assists in beating, whipping, and blending ingredients.

- Fine-Mesh Strainer: This assists in separating the finest mesh from the remainder to accomplish a wonderful finish.

- Ladle: This deep spoon assists in serving foods like soups and stews.

- Tongs: These grippers are employed for flipping, turning, and serving the food.

- Potato Masher: This tool helps convert potatoes or other items into a fine, velvety consistency by mashing them.

- Spatula: This is helpful in turning crepes, pancakes, burgers, and more.

- Colander: This helps to empty the water out of the ingredients, leaving behind the flawlessly drained ingredients.

- Pastry Brush: This brush is used to coat your baking pan and in the coating of other baked items.

2.3 UNDERSTANDING MEASUREMENTS

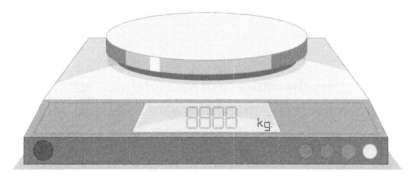

It is exceptionally essential to measure your ingredients properly to make the best dishes and get good results. Always keep in mind that dry and liquid ingredients are measured differently. Remember, only large amounts of liquid and dry items require cups, while small quantities can be measured using measuring spoons.

- Measuring Liquid Ingredients: Every liquid ingredient, from milk and juice to water, must be measured using a liquid measuring cup like a large glass or clear plastic cup with measuring lines on the side and a pour spout and handle. Position your measuring cup over the kitchen counter, then bend down to see the concave arc at the surface of the liquid, known as the meniscus line.

- Measuring Dry Ingredients: Every dry item, from flour, sugar, and rice to fresh or frozen veggies, must be measured using dry measuring cups like small plastic or metal cups with handles. Each set arrives with cups of different sizes, like 1/2 cup, 1/4 cup, 1/3 cup, and 1 cup. Immerse the measuring cup inside the ingredients, and clean and level the excess using the back of a knife.

COOKING MATH

Refrain from letting the intricacy of measurement estimations defeat you. Just remember these straightforward rules, and you are all set!

3 teaspoons = 1 tablespoon

16 tablespoons = 1 cup

16 ounces = 1 pound

So, now that you have understood all the basics and essentials of the kitchen, are you ready to take your steps toward our next chapter? Let's move towards healthy eating habits.

CHAPTER 3: BUILDING HEALTHY HABITS

Welcome, little chefs and their parents! In this chapter, we will explore the world of building healthy habits that will fill up your bodies and satisfy your taste buds. So, prepare yourself to embark on a journey full of flavors where you will discover the wonders of nutrition, explore the happiness of cooking for health, and sprinkle a pinch of creativity into every healthy bite. So, wear your aprons, grab your spoons, and let's beat up some healthy habits together!

3.1 IMPORTANCE OF NUTRITION FOR GROWING KIDS (FOR PARENTS)

Hey, dear parents, do you know that kids require optimal nutrition for their growth, learning, and development? This indicates that you have to incorporate plenty of fruits, veggies, whole grains, and lean protein foods into their diets to make sure that they are receiving all the essential nutrients. The key to nurturing healthy kids and families is to provide tasty, nutrient-rich foods to your kids and encourage them to cook healthy meals, too.

Here are some simple and crucial methods to give your kids nourishing choices from each food group throughout the day, from breakfast to dinner.

1. WHOLE GRAINS

Whole grains are a powerhouse of nutrients, consisting of B vitamins and dietary fiber, and their carbohydrates supply essential fuel for kids' bodies to grow and keep active.

With the group of grain products lining grocery shelves in the past few years, it can be hard to pick the right ones. Always opt for products where whole grains are listed as the primary ingredient on the label. Offer your kids options like whole-grain cold or hot cereals for breakfast, whole-grain crunchy crackers for snacks, and whole-grain pasta for dinner, as these are the nutritious options. To incorporate variety, you can also try quick-fix whole grains like whole-wheat couscous, quinoa, and instant brown rice separately or combined with other ingredients. Similarly, encourage them to cook these items too.

2. FRUITS AND VEGGIES

You can always go right with veggies and fruits, whether they are frozen, fresh, dried, canned, or in the form of juice. Fruits and veggies provide a variety of minerals and vitamins, like potassium, vitamins A, C, and dietary fiber.

Consuming plenty of fruits and veggies is important for the health of kids and grownups alike. At breakfast, your kids can enjoy fresh or frozen fruits like berries on top of cereal or in the form of a smoothie, pieces of melon, a glass of pure juice, or eggs full of veggies. At lunch, kids can have sliced apples or crunchy baby carrots; for dinner, kids can have colored veggies (corn, frozen peas, broccoli, sliced peppers, or leafy green salad) in the middle of every plate. Juice, undoubtedly, is a tasty way to get good nutrients, but it cannot replace the advantages of consuming whole veggies and fruits, so aim to derive at least half of the fruit options from whole fruits for your kids.

3. LOW-FAT DAIRY ITEMS

For kids, dairy foods are a rich source of calcium, protein, phosphorus, and magnesium, all of which are essential for kids. Many children or even grownups around the world need to consume sufficient amounts of potassium or calcium. Getting the important nutrients for kids is, fortunately, a breeze with 3 daily servings of dairy. Try to incorporate low-fat and nutrient-rich dairy products into your child's daily routine. Options can be an 8-ounce glass of low-fat milk along with each meal, low-fat parfaits at breakfast or as a snack, and string cheese for a rapid energy boost.

4. LEAN MEAT, POULTRY, EGGS, FISH, NUTS, OR BEANS

When it comes to building strong muscles or an active brain, this distinct group of foods not only has protein but also provides essential nutrients like zinc, iron, and B vitamins that are extremely important for a kid's growth. Ensuring an adequate intake of protein during every meal and snack can result in prolonged satiety, leaving kids feeling comfortably satisfied after eating.

Many kids consume the right amount of protein during lunch and dinner but may fall short of their protein requirements during snacks or breakfast. In the morning, yogurt, eggs, and breakfast burritos are great options. When it comes to snacking, nut butter, hummus, peanut butter, nuts, or other bean dips are great choices for kids.

3.2 PROMOTE HEALTHY HABITS IN KIDS THROUGH COOKING AND MEAL PREP (FOR PARENTS)

Promoting healthy eating patterns in kids is vital for their overall health, and one effective approach to instilling these habits is through meal preparation and cooking. Here is how:

1. GET KIDS INVOLVED IN MEAL PLANNING

- Motivate kids to take part in meal planning by asking about their intake and making menu suggestions. Please take into account their preferences and integrate them into the meal plan.

- Bring your kids along when you go grocery shopping and involve them in choosing lean proteins, whole grains, fresh produce, and other healthy ingredients.

2. PRACTICAL COOKING EXPERIENCE

- Motivate kids to actively engage in cooking adventures that match their abilities and ages. These tasks may include stirring ingredients, washing veggies, or assembling sandwiches.

- Opt for easy recipes featuring simple-to-follow instructions that are easily understandable for kids. Seek out recipes particularly tailored for children or adapt grownup recipes to guarantee they are more enjoyable and accessible for little chefs.

3. PROVIDE THEM INFORMATION ABOUT NUTRITION

- Take advantage of meal preparation and cooking moments to educate kids about the nutritional advantages of different foods. Engage in discussions about the importance of consuming a different range of foods from every food category in order to sustain optimal health.

- Describe the advantages of incorporating nutrient-dense foods, such as veggies, fruits, lean proteins, whole grains, etc., into a diet. It is necessary to enlighten kids on the ways in which these foods provide their bodies with vital minerals, vitamins, and the energy they require to thrive.

4. BUILD A POSITIVE COOKING ATMOSPHERE

- Cultivate an atmosphere in the kitchen that is both uplifting and supportive, allowing kids to feel comfortable when exploring new flavors and trying out various cooking methods.

- Highlight the pleasure derived from preparing dishes and the satisfaction that comes from making delectable and healthy dishes together as a family.

5. HIGHLIGHT THE SIGNIFICANCE OF BALANCE AND PRACTICING MODERATION

- Instill in kids the comprehension of balance and moderation when it comes to their food choices. Foster a mindset that welcomes a diverse range of foods, all the while being mindful of appropriate portion sizes.

- Talk about the significance of including occasional treats and indulgences in moderation within a well-rounded diet.

6. DISCOVER A WIDE RANGE OF CUISINES

- Expose kids to different culinary traditions from various parts of the world. Go on a journey to explore unfamiliar, unique tastes and creative cooking methods as a team.

- Utilize cooking as a means to encourage kids to discover a variety of cuisines and flavors.

7. CELEBRATE KIDS' ACCOMPLISHMENTS

- Take time to acknowledge and celebrate the accomplishments of kids in the kitchen. This could include trying an unfamiliar food, learning a new cooking technique, or successfully preparing a dish on their own. It is crucial to praise their struggles and give them praise while also motivating them to proceed with their culinary experimentation and exploration.

By involving kids in the process of meal preparation and cooking, we not only equip them with essential life skills, but also instill in them the knowledge to make healthy choices and develop a never-ending appreciation for nutritious foods.

So, finally, the time to step up in the kitchen and start making your favorite food has arrived. So, little chefs, put on your chef's hat, wear your apron, get your cooking tools ready, and let the cooking adventure begin.

CHAPTER 4: BREAKFAST RECIPES

Note: It is crucial to remember that kids between the ages of 4-6 years are still growing and may be too immature to handle specific kitchen tasks, like cutting with knives, operating stoves, and ovens, handling hot surfaces, etc. As a result, most of the recipes require adult supervision, and therefore, parents are requested to help out their kids during the cooking process to ensure their safety.

1. SIMPLE SCRAMBLED EGGS

Serves: 4 | Prep Time: 10 minutes | Cooking Time: 15 minutes | Difficulty Level: Medium

INGREDIENTS:

- 4 tablespoons of butter
- Kosher salt
- 6 to 8 eggs
- Freshly ground black pepper
- Flake salt, like Maldon, for finishing

TASTY ADD-ONS:

- Bacon or ham
- Sautéed mushrooms or broccoli
- Minced chives or scallions
- Shredded cheese, folded in or finely shredded to top
- Diced tomatoes

EQUIPMENT:

- Heat-tolerant rubber spatula
- Whisk
- Small bowl
- Medium sauté pan

INSTRUCTIONS:

- Break the eggs into a small-sized bowl and whisk them until they are frothy. Season with pepper and salt.

- Melt the butter in a medium-sized pan on a medium flame, and then turn the flame to low as the butter heats up. Pour the whisked eggs into the pan and allow them to cook for a few seconds.

- Using a spatula, nudge and mix the eggs, constantly scraping the bottom of the pan as you mix them around the pan to avoid sticking. With a spatula, move the eggs from the center out, and then scrape the edges of the pan, and swirl the outermost eggs toward the middle. Proceed to do this until the eggs look like pudding, and then make them into dense egg curds for about 4 minutes.

- If you want to include add-ons, add them after adding the egg and when it lightly starts becoming stiff.

- Serve and enjoy.

2. FRUIT SMOOTHIE

Serves: 4 | Prep Time: 10 minutes | Cooking Time: 0 minutes | Difficulty Level: Easy

INGREDIENTS:

- 1 cup of whole milk

- 3/4 cup of frozen or fresh blueberries

- 1 teaspoon of vanilla extract (optional)

- 3 bananas (sliced)

- 2 cups of thick, plain yogurt

EQUIPMENT:

- Small, sharp knife

- Blender

- Cutting board

- First, start by peeling the bananas, and then chop them into small chunks. Add the banana chunks into the blender, then add yogurt, blueberries, milk, and vanilla extract.

- Pulse the blender until the combination is thick, smooth, and creamy. Pour the smoothie into serving glasses, and enjoy this nutritious and simple breakfast.

3. BANANA PANCAKES

Serves: 4 | Prep Time: 10 minutes | Cooking Time: 20 minutes | Difficulty Level: Medium

INGREDIENTS:

- 2 bananas (peeled)

- 3/4 cup of milk

- 1 egg

- 3/4 cup of self-rising flour

- Butter (for frying)

- 2 tablespoons of sugar

- 1/3 cup of self-rising whole wheat flour

EQUIPMENT:

- Large non-stick frying pan
- Sieve
- Wooden spoon
- Fork or masher
- Measuring cup
- 2 bowls
- Ladle
- Spatula
- Whisk or fork

INSTRUCTIONS:

- Sift together both the flours in a mixing bowl. Add in the sugar and create a well in the center of the mixture.

- Now, put the milk and egg together in a mixing cup and mix them until they are entirely mixed. Pour the combination into the well in the center of the flour and sugar. Using a wooden spoon, beat until you have a smooth and creamy batter.

- Let the batter rest for about 30 minutes. Mash bananas into a bowl and incorporate them into the batter.

- Melt a dash of butter in a pan. Add three small spoonfuls of batter to create 2 pancakes, each around 3 1/2 inches (8 centimeters) in diameter.

- Cook them for around 2 minutes or until bubbles occur over the surface. Flip the pancakes and cook for another 2 minutes to make both sides equally golden brown.

- Repeat the process with the remaining batter.

- Serve with a drizzle of honey, and enjoy.

4. STRAWBERRY YOGURT CRUNCH

Serves: 2 | Prep Time: 10 minutes | Cooking Time: 5 minutes | Difficulty Level: Easy

INGREDIENTS:

- 2/3 cup of whole oats

- 1 cup of whole strawberries (about 6 to 8)

- 12 teaspoons of thick, plain yogurt

- 4 tablespoons of fresh orange juice

- 3 tablespoons of sunflower seeds

- 2 to 3 tablespoons of clear, runny honey

- 3 tablespoons of pumpkin seeds

EQUIPMENT:

- Cutting board
- Frying pan
- Small, sharp knife
- Small bowl
- Wooden spoon

INSTRUCTIONS:

- Remove the leaves and stems of strawberries, and then cut them into slices. Add the strawberries to a mixing bowl and pour the orange juice over them. Set them aside for now.

- Add the oats to a hot frying pan and toast them for about 3 minutes on medium to low flame. Turn the oats occasionally using a wooden spoon to ensure they are cooking evenly.

- Now, add the pumpkin and sunflower seeds and toast for an additional 2 minutes or until golden brown. Take care — as the pumpkin seeds may pop a bit.

- Take the pan off the flame. Mix in the honey; it will sizzle initially, but keep mixing until the seeds and oats are coated. Allow to slightly cool.

- Create a layer of oats in the base of each glass, then add 2 heaped spoonfuls of yogurt and some of the fruit above. Make another layer following the same procedure.

- Serve and enjoy.

5. NUT AND FRUIT BREAKFAST BOWL

Serves: 4 | Prep Time: 10 minutes | Cooking Time: 0 minutes | Difficulty Level: Easy

INGREDIENTS:

- ½ cup of unsweetened coconut flakes, toasted
- 4 tablespoons of peanut butter
- 2 tablespoons of chia seeds
- 4 tablespoons of flax meal
- 2 tablespoons of nuts, toasted and coarsely chopped, like pistachios or almonds
- 2 cups of Greek yogurt
- 3 cups of fresh fruit, like pomegranate, raspberries, seeds, blueberries, persimmon, apples, or pears

EQUIPMENT:

- Spoon
- Mixing bowl
- Serving bowls

INSTRUCTIONS:

- Mix the yogurt until creamy and smooth. Divide the yogurt into bowls. Sprinkle flax meal and chia seeds into each. First, add the peanut butter, and next, the fruit.

- Sprinkle the chopped nuts and toasted coconut into each bowl to finish the dish.

- Serve and eat immediately.

CHAPTER 5: LIGHT MEAL RECIPES

Note: It is crucial to remember that kids between the ages of 4-6 years are still growing and may be too immature to handle specific kitchen tasks, like cutting with knives, operating stoves and ovens, handling hot surfaces, etc. As a result, most of the recipes require adult supervision, and therefore, parents are requested to help out their kids during the cooking process to ensure their safety.

1. CORN CHOWDER

Serves: 4 | Prep Time: 15 minutes | Cooking Time: 30 minutes | Difficulty Level: Medium

INGREDIENTS:

- 1 1/4 cups of milk
- 1 large onion
- 1 cup of frozen, fresh, or canned sweet corn
- 3/4 lb. (350g) of potatoes

- 1 bay leaf

- 1 tablespoon of sunflower oil

- 3 sprigs of thyme (optional)

- 1 large carrot

- 3 sprigs of parsley (optional)

- 5 cups of vegetable stock

- Salt and black pepper

EQUIPMENT:

- Large saucepan with lid

- Small, sharp knife

- Wooden spoon

- Cutting board

- Vegetable peeler

- Blender

INSTRUCTIONS:

- Roughly chop the onion after peeling it. Slice the carrot after peeling it, and finally, cut the potato into small chunks after peeling it.

- Add oil to the saucepan and let it heat. Add the onion and sauté for around 8 minutes on a medium flame until slightly golden and soft. Occasionally, stir the onion.

- Next, add the carrot, corn, potatoes, parsley, thyme, and bay leaf to the onions. Cook for a further 2 minutes, stirring frequently. Pour the stock and bring it to the boiling point.

- Reduce the flame to medium-low and cover using a lid. Cook for around 15 more minutes, occasionally stirring. Add the milk and cook for an additional 5 minutes.

- Take out some of the veggies and blend the remainder of the soup until creamy. Return the veggies and blended soup mixture to the pan and warm for some more minutes.

- Take the soup out in the serving bowls.

- Serve and enjoy.

2. SUMMERY CORN AND WATERMELON SALAD

Serves: 4 | Prep Time: 10 minutes | Cooking Time: 0 minutes | Difficulty Level: Easy

INGREDIENTS:

- 5 fresh basil leaves

- Flake salt, like Maldon

- 1/4 teaspoon of ground cayenne

- 2 ears of fresh sweet corn, cooked and cut off cob

- 1 teaspoon of ground sumac
- 1/2 small watermelon, seeded, rind extracted, cut into one-inch cubes
- Zest of ½ lemon

- Zester
- Serving platter

INSTRUCTIONS:

- Add the cubed watermelon with its juices to a serving platter. Now, add the corn cut from the cobs. Sprinkle the cayenne and sumac over the top of the watermelon and corn; next, add the lemon zest.

- Now, finally, slice the basil. Do this quickly prior to serving salad because the edges will darken from cutting (called oxidation). Pile the basil leaves together and make a tight bundle. Using your knife, slice them and create skinny strips (known as chiffonade).

- Now separate the basil chiffonade and add it on top of the salad.

- Season with salt and serve immediately.

3. BAKED EGGS AND HAM

Serves: 2 to 4 | Prep Time: 10 minutes | Cooking Time: 15 minutes | Difficulty Level: Medium

INGREDIENTS:

- 4 slices of lean ham
- A little olive oil
- 4 eggs

EQUIPMENT:

- Small spatula
- Pastry brush
- Kitchen scissors
- Small bowl
- Muffin tin
- Oven mitts

INSTRUCTIONS:

- Preheat your oven to 400°F. Lightly coat 4 holes of a large muffin tin with a brush using oil. This step will stop the ham from sticking to the tin.

- Add the slice of ham in every hole. Carefully trim the extra part hanging out of the top to make them even, but remember that the ham should be a bit above the edge of the muffin tin.

- One by one, beat eggs into a bowl and add them to a ham-lined tin, one egg in each hole. Bake for around 10 to 15 minutes in the oven, or until the egg is cooked.

- Take the muffin tin out of the oven with the help of oven mitts, and allow it to cool for some time.

- Now, carefully lift out the muffins using a small spatula.

- Serve and enjoy.

4. CARROT SOUP

Serves: 1 to 2 | Prep Time: 10 minutes | Cooking Time: 30 minutes | Difficulty Level: Medium

INGREDIENTS:

- 1 (1-inch) piece of fresh ginger, peeled and chopped

- 1/4 teaspoon of salt

- 1/3 cup of milk

- 8 ounces of carrots, peeled and cut into 1-inch pieces

- 1 1/3 cups of chicken or vegetable broth

- 1 tablespoon of vegetable oil

EQUIPMENT:

- Ladle
- 1 or 2 bowls or mugs
- Oven mitts
- Wooden spoon
- Large saucepan with lid
- Blender
- Dish towel

INSTRUCTIONS:

- In a large-sized saucepan, heat oil on a medium flame for around 1 minute. Add carrots, ginger, and salt and cook; mix occasionally using a wooden spoon for around 5 minutes or until light brown.

- Add the broth and increase the flame to high. Let it boil. Decrease the flame to medium-low and simmer after covering until the carrots are smooth, for about 15 minutes. Turn the flame off and put the saucepan on the cool side of the stove. Remove the lid using oven mitts and permit it to cool for about 5 minutes.

- Add the soup to a blender jar carefully, using a spoon. Pour milk and put the lid on the blender. Tightly hold it in place with a folded dish towel. Blend until smooth and creamy, for about 1 minute. Add the soup to serving bowls.

- Serve and enjoy.

5. COLORFUL SHRIMP SALAD

Serves: 4 | Prep Time: 15 minutes | Cooking Time: 12 minutes | Difficulty Level: Easy

INGREDIENTS:

- 1 large avocado
- 1 cup of cooked and peeled shrimp
- 3/4 cup of pasta shells
- 12 small tomatoes (quartered)
- Lettuce leaves (cut into strips)

DRESSING:

- 2 teaspoons of lemon juice
- 4 tablespoons of mayonnaise
- 2 tablespoons of ketchup
- Salt and pepper
- 2 drops of Tabasco sauce (optional)

EQUIPMENT:

- Large saucepan
- Small spoon
- Wooden spoon
- Small, sharp knife
- Mixing bowl
- Cutting board
- Small bowl

INSTRUCTIONS:

- Add water to a large-sized saucepan and bring it to a boil. Once boiling, add pasta and cook according to package instructions.

- Drain out well and leave aside to cool. Meanwhile, cut the avocado around its center and carefully pry it apart. Take out the pit using a small spoon, then cut every half into quarters.

- Peel the skin off and cut the avocado into cubes. Transfer the avocado to a bowl and add half of the lemon juice on top of it to stop it from turning brown.

- Now, put the avocado, shrimp, and tomatoes into a bowl with the pasta and mix. Distribute the lettuce leaves between the serving bowls.

- Combine all the dressing ingredients inside a small cup. Add the shrimp salad to the serving bowls and add the dressing on top of it.

- Serve and enjoy.

CHAPTER 6: SNACKS AND DRINKS RECIPES

Note: It is crucial to remember that kids between the ages of 4-6 years are still growing and may be too immature to handle specific kitchen tasks, like cutting with knives, operating stoves and ovens, handling hot surfaces, etc. As a result, most of the recipes require adult supervision, and therefore, parents are requested to help out their kids during the cooking process to ensure their safety.

1. TROPICAL MOCKTAIL

Serves: 1 | Prep Time: 5 minutes | Cooking Time: 0 minutes | Difficulty Level: Easy

INGREDIENTS:

- 2 tablespoons of 100% cranberry juice
- ½ cup club soda
- 2 tablespoons of pineapple juice
- Ice cubes
- 1 tablespoon of orange juice concentrate

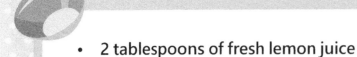

- 2 tablespoons of fresh lemon juice

- Mixing spoon
- Tall drinking glass
- Measuring cup
- Fancy straw (optional)
- Measuring spoons

INSTRUCTIONS:

- First, start by adding the ice to the glass. Remember, the ideal glass will be see-through so that you can observe all the colors.
- Now prepare the drink. Add the cranberry juice, lemon juice, orange juice concentrate, club soda, and pineapple juice over the ice. Mix using a spoon and add a fancy straw to add a touch of creativity if you have one.

2. PARMESAN PITA CHIPS

Serves: 3 to 4 | Prep Time: 5 minutes | Cooking Time: 10 minutes | Difficulty Level: Easy

INGREDIENTS:

- 1/2 cup of grated Parmesan cheese
- 6 tablespoons of oil

- 4 pieces of pita bread
- 1 1/2 tablespoons of sesame seeds

- Cookie sheet
- Small bowl
- Pizza cutter
- Serving platter

- Preheat your oven to 425°F.
- Divide every pita bread in half and cut each half into 3 wedges using a pizza cutter.
- Set wedges on a cookie sheet.
- Mix together the sesame seeds and parmesan cheese in a small-sized bowl.
- Cover the outer side of each pita wedge using oil.
- Spread the parmesan-sesame mixture over the pita wedges.
- Bake until light golden brown, for about 5 to 10 minutes.

3. CARROT AND APPLE JUICE

Serves: 2 | Prep Time: 5 minutes | Cooking Time: 0 minutes | Difficulty Level: Easy

INGREDIENTS:

- 4 apples
- Squeeze of fresh lemon juice (optional)
- 3 carrots

EQUIPMENT:

- Cutting board
- Small, sharp knife
- Juicer

INSTRUCTIONS:

- Start by scrubbing the carrots and cutting each into small pieces. Extract the stems from the apples and cut them into quarters carefully.

- Run the carrots and apples through the juicer. Discard the pulp and pour the juice into 2 glasses. Add a squeeze of lemon and mix the juice.

- Serve and enjoy.

4. TREASURE TRAIL MIX

Serves: 2 | Prep Time: 5 minutes | Cooking Time: 0 minutes | Difficulty Level: Easy

- 1/2 cup of raisins

- 1/4 cup of chocolate chips

- 1/2 cup of small pretzel twists or sticks

- 1/4 cup of sunflower seeds

- 1/2 cup of peanuts

EQUIPMENT:

- Airtight container

- Large bowl

INSTRUCTIONS:

- Add all the ingredients to a large-sized bowl and mix together until well combined.

- Serve the trail mix and enjoy.

- Transfer the leftovers to an airtight container and store them in a cool and dry place.

5. TOMATO AND MOZZARELLA BITES

Serves: 2 to 4 | Prep Time: 10 minutes | Cooking Time: 0 minutes | Difficulty Level: Easy

INGREDIENTS:

- 8 baby mozzarella balls

- Salt and pepper

- 8 fresh, small basil leaves

- 1 tablespoon of extra-virgin olive oil

- 8 grape or cherry tomatoes

EQUIPMENT:

- Cutting board

- Medium bowl

- Rubber spatula

- 8 sturdy wooden toothpicks, each around 3 inches' long

- Paring knife

INSTRUCTIONS:

- Start by slicing the tomatoes in half and adding them to a medium-sized bowl. Next, add the mozzarella balls and coat them with oil. Sprinkle with pepper and salt and gently toss with the help of a rubber spatula.

- Thread the tomato half onto a wooden toothpick. Now, thread the basil leaf on top of the tomato, then thread the mozzarella ball onto a toothpick. Finish the skewers by threading the other tomato half onto the end.

- Serve and have fun.

6. TANGY ORANGE FIZZ

Serves: 2 | Prep Time: 10 minutes | Cooking Time: 0 minutes | Difficulty Level: Easy

INGREDIENTS:

- 1 cup of lemonade
- 1 cup of orange juice
- 1 cup of sparkling water

EQUIPMENT:

- Serving glasses
- Pitcher

INSTRUCTIONS:

- Add all the ingredients in a large pitcher.
- Mix well.
- Add into serving glasses.
- Serve and enjoy.

CHAPTER 7: MAIN MEAL RECIPES

Note: It is crucial to remember that kids between the ages of 4-6 years are still growing and may be too immature to handle specific kitchen tasks, like cutting with knives, operating stoves and ovens, handling hot surfaces, etc. As a result, most of the recipes require adult supervision, and therefore, parents are requested to help out their kids during the cooking process to ensure their safety.

1. ONE SHEET CHICKEN FAJITAS

Serves: 4 | Prep Time: 10 minutes | Cooking Time: 30 minutes | Difficulty Level: Medium

INGREDIENTS:

- 8 small tortillas (corn or flour)
- Olive oil cooking spray
- 3 bell peppers (any color)
- 1 ½ pounds of boneless and skinless chicken breasts

- 3 teaspoons of taco seasoning

- 1 teaspoon of kosher salt

- 1 ½ tablespoons of olive oil

- 1 small red onion

EQUIPMENT:

- Cutting board

- Baking sheet

- Meat thermometer

- Kid-safe knife

- Mixing bowl

- Aluminum foil

- Measuring spoons

INSTRUCTIONS:

- Preheat your oven to 425°F. Line the baking sheet with aluminum foil. Coat the foil using the olive oil.

- Cut the chicken into 1/2-inch thick strips and add them to a mixing bowl. Now, cut the bell pepper into 1/2-inch thick strips. Next, cut the onion into 1/4-inch thick strips. Place the prepared veggies into the mixing bowl.

- In the bowl of chicken, put the taco seasoning, olive oil, and salt. Mix well.

- Spread the veggie and chicken mixture in a single, uniform layer on the coated baking sheet. Transfer the baking sheet to the oven and bake for about 20 minutes or until the chicken is cooked through (the chicken should register 160°F when checked with a meat thermometer).

- Take the sheet pan out of the oven. Allow it to cool for around 10 minutes prior to eating. Serve and enjoy; you can eat it with tortillas.

2. LAVASH SANDWICH ROLL-UP

Serves: 2 | Prep Time: 10 minutes | Cooking Time: 0 minutes | Difficulty Level: Easy

INGREDIENTS:

- 1/4 cup of chopped raisins or dried cranberries
- 1/2 medium apple (your favorite kind)
- 1/4 cup of Cheerios (or other cereal of your preference)
- 1 lavash flatbread (or tortilla, pita, naan, or other flatbread)
- 1/4 cup of seed or nut butter (your favorite kind)
- Pinch of ground cinnamon
- 1/4 cup of toasted sunflower seeds

EQUIPMENT:

- Cutting board
- Measuring cup
- Kid-safe knife

INSTRUCTIONS:

- Firstly, cut an apple in half and extract the core. Then, cut the apple and make matchsticks out of it.

- Lay the bread out and spread seed or nut butter over the surface of the bread.

- Now is the time to add the toppings. Put the apple matchsticks down the middle of the prepared lavash lengthwise. Scatter the seeds, raisins, and cereal over the apple matchsticks. Dust using the cinnamon.

- Now, make the roll by folding up the lavash lengthwise. Slice the roll in half.

- Serve the rolls immediately or tightly wrap them using plastic wrap and refrigerate for later use.

3. ROASTED TOMATO AND CORN TOSTADAS

Serves: 2 to 4 | Prep Time: 10 minutes | Cooking Time: 35 minutes | Difficulty Level: Hard

INGREDIENTS:

- 1/2 cup of frozen corn
- 1/2 cup of refried beans
- 1/2 teaspoon of chili powder (optional)
- 2 1/2 cups of cherry tomatoes, cut in half
- 1/4 teaspoon of salt
- 1/4 cup of fresh cilantro leaves
- 4 (6- inch) corn tostadas
- 1/2 cup of crumbled feta cheese or queso fresco
- 1 tablespoon plus 1 teaspoon of vegetable oil, measured separately

EQUIPMENT:

- Rimmed baking sheet
- Medium bowl
- Spatula
- Large spoon
- Rubber spatula
- 13-by-9-inch baking dish
- Oven mitts
- Plates

- Small bowl
- Cooling rack
- Small spoon

INSTRUCTIONS:

- Position the oven rack to low-middle rank and position the temperature of the oven to 400°F.

- Put tomatoes, chili powder, 1 tablespoon of oil, corn, and salt in a medium-sized bowl and mix using a rubber spatula until incorporated.

- Add the tomato mixture to baking dish. Move the baking dish to the oven and bake for about 20 to 25 minutes or until the tomatoes are soft.

- Meanwhile, mix the remaining 1 teaspoon of oil with the refried beans in a small-sized bowl until smooth. Distribute beans uniformly over tostadas using the back of a spoon. Put tostadas on a rimmed baking sheet.

- Remove the baking dish from the oven with the help of oven mitts and transfer it to the cooling rack.

- Using a large spoon, add the tomato mixture uniformly over tostadas. Place the baking sheet in the oven and then bake tostadas for about 5 minutes or until the beans are warmed through.

- Remove the baking sheet out of the oven using oven mitts and shift it to the cooling rack. Scatter cheese and cilantro over the top. Carefully move tostadas to serving plates utilizing a spatula.

- Serve and enjoy.

4. TUNA NOODLE CASSEROLE

Serves: 4 | Prep Time: 10 minutes | Cooking Time: 35 minutes | Difficulty Level: Medium

INGREDIENTS:

- 1 cup of milk

- 2 (6-ounce) cans of tuna fish in water, drained

- ¼ cup of fried onions for topping

- 6 ounces of egg noodles

- 1 (10¾-ounce) can cream of mushroom soup

EQUIPMENT:

- Saucepan

- 2-quart casserole dish

- Spoon

- Large bowl

INSTRUCTIONS:

- Preheat your oven to 375°F. Grease a 2-quart casserole dish with cooking spray.

- Prepare the egg noodles by following the instructions on the package and drain them.

- Add together the mushroom soup, drained tuna, cooked noodles, and milk in a large-sized bowl and mix well.

- Shift the tuna mixture into a greased casserole dish and sprinkle the fried onions.

- Transfer the casserole dish to the oven and bake for about 25 to 30 minutes.

- Once cooked, take the dish out of the oven, let it cool slightly, and then serve.

5. VEGGIE BURGERS

Serves: 2 | Prep Time: 10 minutes | Cooking Time: 20 minutes | Difficulty Level: Hard

INGREDIENTS:

- 4 hamburger buns

- 1 (15-ounce) can of chickpeas

- 3 scallions, thinly sliced

- 1/2 teaspoon of curry powder

- 2 tablespoons of plain Greek yogurt, plus additional for serving
- 1/3 cup of panko bread crumbs
- 2 teaspoons plus 2 teaspoons of olive oil (extra-virgin), separately measured
- 1/8 teaspoon of salt
- 4 leaves of lettuce
- 1 large egg
- A pinch of pepper

EQUIPMENT:

- Medium bowl
- 10- inch non-stick skillet
- Spatula
- Food processor
- 3/4-cup dry measuring cup
- Whisk
- Colander
- Rubber spatula
- Can opener
- Ruler

INSTRUCTIONS:

- Set your colander in the sink. Open the chickpea can and place it in the colander.

- Rinse the chickpeas under cold water and shake the colander to remove the water. Keep 3/4 cup for now and reserve the other amount for later use.

- Whisk together the egg, yogurt, curry powder, egg, 2 teaspoons of oil, and pepper in a medium-sized bowl until well mixed.

- Now, add the scallions, panko, and 3/4 cup of chickpeas to a food processor. Place the lid on. Pulse for around one second, and then stop. Repeat the procedure (around 6 to 8 pulses) until everything is chopped with a few bigger chunks remaining.

- Transfer the chickpea mixture to a bowl, and add the egg mixture on top of it. Carefully mix the ingredients with the help of a rubber spatula until thoroughly mixed.

- Now evenly distribute the mixture into 2 balls using your hands. Slightly flatten every ball to create a circle of 4 inches across.

- Put 2 remaining teaspoons of oil into a non-stick skillet and spin the skillet to coat it with oil equally. Add patties to the skillet and cook on medium flame until lightly golden brown on the side for about 5 to 6 minutes.

- Carefully turn the patties using a spatula. Now cook on the opposite side until well browned, for around 4 to 5 minutes. Turn the flame off.

- Now, start by layering the lettuce leaf on a bun. Put the patties into the buns with a spatula. Serve with your preferred toppings and enjoy.

CHAPTER 8: DESSERTS RECIPES

Note: It is crucial to remember that kids between the ages of 4-6 years are still growing and may be too immature to handle specific kitchen tasks, like cutting with knives, operating stoves and ovens, handling hot surfaces, etc. As a result, most of the recipes require adult supervision, and therefore, parents are requested to help out their kids during the cooking process to ensure their safety.

1. FROZEN YOGURT BARK

Serves: 4 | Prep Time: 10 minutes | Cooking Time: 0 minutes | Difficulty Level: Easy

INGREDIENTS:

- 1/2 teaspoon of pure vanilla extract

- 2 cups of full-fat Greek yogurt (or a non-dairy alternative)

- ½ teaspoon of lemon zest

- 2 tablespoons of pure maple syrup

- 1/2 cup toppings of your choice: sliced strawberries, crushed nuts, blueberries, shredded coconut, cranberries, raisins, dark chocolate shavings, and hulled hemp seeds

EQUIPMENT:

- Mixing spoon
- Medium mixing bowl
- Sharp knife
- Measuring cup
- Rimmed baking sheet
- Measuring spoon
- Wax paper

INSTRUCTIONS:

- Combine the maple syrup, yogurt, and vanilla in a medium-sized bowl.
- Line the rimmed baking sheet with wax paper.
- Add the yogurt mixture to a lined baking sheet and evenly spread (make sure it is just around 1/2 inch in thickness).
- Now sprinkle your selected toppings over the top of the yogurt mixture.
- Transfer the pan to the freezer and freeze for about 2 to 4 hours until the bark is hardened.
- Before serving, break the bark into cubes using a sharp knife.
- Serve and enjoy.

2. TASTY FUDGE

Serves: 2 dozen | Prep Time: 15 minutes | Cooking Time: 10 minutes | Difficulty Level: Medium

INGREDIENTS:

- 3 (12-ounce) packages of chocolate chips
- 1 ½ sticks of butter or margarine
- 1 (7 ½-ounce) jar of marshmallow cream
- 2/3 cup of evaporated milk
- 3 cups of sugar
- 1 teaspoon of vanilla

EQUIPMENT:

- Spatula
- Saucepan
- Baking pan
- Spoon
- Measuring cup

INSTRUCTIONS:

- Grease a 9" × 13" pan using cooking spray.
- Add the sugar, butter, and milk to a large-sized pan.

- Heat the combination until it boils. Frequently stir. (It will take approximately. 5 minutes)

- Turn the flame off and remove the pan from the stove.

- Fold in the chocolate chips and mix until melted.

- Mix in the remainder of the ingredients and mix until everything is well combined.

- Layer the fudge mixture on a coated baking pan.

- Refrigerate until the fudge hardens (about 4 hours).

- After the fudge is set, take it out of the refrigerator, then slice and serve.

3. RASPBERRY LEMON MUG CAKE

Serves: 1 | Prep Time: 5 minutes | Cooking Time: 5 minutes | Difficulty Level: Easy

INGREDIENTS:

- 1 tablespoon of raspberry jam

- 2 tablespoons of white sugar

- ¼ teaspoon of baking powder

- 2 teaspoons of full-fat sour cream

- 1 teaspoon of softened, unsalted butter

- 2 tablespoons of whole milk or a non-dairy alternative

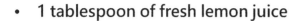

- 1 tablespoon of fresh lemon juice

- 3 tablespoons of all-purpose flour

- ¼ teaspoon of pure vanilla extract

EQUIPMENT:

- Measuring spoons

- Chopstick or fork

- Microwave-safe coffee mug

INSTRUCTIONS:

- Take a mug and add sugar, flour, and baking powder to it. Stir well using a small fork or chopstick.

- Now, add the butter, lemon juice, sour cream, milk, and vanilla to the mug. Mix until well combined; make sure to utilize a fork or chopstick to get any ingredients that may be stuck around the base of the mug.

- On top of the batter, add a spoonful of raspberry jam. Using the fork or chopstick, gently stir to swirl it into batter 2 to 3 times.

- Transfer the mug to the microwave and cook on High for around 1 1/2 minutes. Carefully take the mug out of the microwave. Let it cool for a few minutes before serving.

- Serve and enjoy.

4. MINI TRIFLE

Serves: 2 | Prep Time: 10 minutes | Cooking Time: 0 minutes | Difficulty Level: Easy

INGREDIENTS:

- 8 strawberries, sliced
- 2 bananas
- 1/2 cup of blueberries
- 4 slices of pound cake, cut into cubes
- 1 cup of nondairy whipped topping

EQUIPMENT:

- Spoons
- Trifle glass bowl

INSTRUCTIONS:

- Take a trifle bowl to assemble your trifle.
- Start by layering the pound cake first, then whipped topping, and in the end, fruit as you like them around the bowl.
- Remember to keep 2 tablespoons of topping and strawberry slices aside to add on the top.
- Complete with reserved strawberry slices and whipped topping.

- Serve and enjoy.

5. COCONUT PINEAPPLE POPSICLES

Serves: 6 popsicles | Prep Time: 15 minutes | Cooking Time: 0 minutes | Difficulty Level: Easy

INGREDIENTS:

- 1 cup (7 ounces) of frozen pineapple chunks, thawed
- 3 tablespoons of honey
- 1 teaspoon of grated lime zest plus 1 tablespoon of juice (zested and
- squeezed from half a lime)
- ¼ teaspoon of salt
- 1 (14-ounce) can of coconut milk

EQUIPMENT:

- 6 ice pop molds, about 3 ounces each
- 4-cup liquid measuring cup
- Blender
- 6 ice pop sticks
- Dishtowel
- Large bowl
- Rubber spatula

- Fine-mesh strainer

INSTRUCTIONS:

- Add all of the ingredients to a blender jar. Place the lid over the top of the blender, and tightly hold the lid using a folded dish towel. Blend until thoroughly combined, for about 30 seconds.

- Stop the blender and scrape the sides down with a rubber spatula. Place the lid on and continue processing until smooth and creamy, for about 30 seconds.

- Position a fine-mesh strainer over a large-sized bowl. Pass the coconut-pineapple combination through a strainer into a bowl. Press the mixture with a rubber spatula to pass the liquid via a strainer inside a bowl. Dump the solids.

- Transfer the coconut and pineapple mixture to a liquid measuring cup. Fill the ice pop molds, place them in the freezer, and freeze until they harden, about 8 hours or up to 5 days.

- Once prepared to serve, keep each mold under hot, running water for 20 seconds to soften lightly.

- Remove the popsicles from the mold and serve.

MEASUREMENT CONVERSION TABLE

CUPS	OUNCES	MILLILETERS	TABLESPOONS
8 cups	64 oz.	1895 ml	128
6 cups	48 oz.	1420 ml	96
5 cups	40 oz.	1180 ml	80
4 cups	32 oz.	960 ml	64
2 cups	16 oz.	480 ml	32
1 cup	8 oz.	240 ml	16
3/4 cup	6 oz.	177 ml	12
2/3 cup	5 oz.	158 ml	11
1/2 cup	4 oz.	118 ml	8
3/8 cup	3 oz.	90 ml	6
1/3 cup	2.5 oz.	79 ml	5.5
1/4 cup	2 oz.	59 ml	4
1/8 cup	1 oz.	30 ml	3
1/16 cup	1/2 oz.	15 ml	1

CONCLUSION

As we arrive at the final pages of this cookbook, let us recall all the unforgettable memories made and lessons learned during this cooking journey. In the amusing journey of "My First Cookbook Easy Recipes for Kids Ages 4-6," little chefs have not only discovered the marvels of the kitchen but have also embarked on a delectable adventure of cultivating healthy habits through eating and cooking. From learning simple recipes to learning hard ones, each dish has served as a stepping stone towards cooking creativity and wholesome eating. But our kitchen journey does not end here; it is the beginning of a lifelong passion. So, little ones, let's carry the spirit of exploration and experimentation into every kitchen adventure. Whether it's making a quick scrambled egg for breakfast or preparing snacks for the family, may the skills obtained from this cookbook continue to motivate our little chefs to embrace a lifelong fondness for cooking.So, best of luck for a future full of healthy eating, joyful cooking, and endless culinary experiences!

Made in the USA
Monee, IL
23 November 2024

71023578R00052